Faith

A Bible Study on Ju....

Keri Folmar
Cruciform Press | February 2014

To my grandmother, Ruth Elizabeth Oates,
a steadfast woman of faith characterized by joy.

– Keri Folmar

CruciformPress

"Keri Folmar encourages us to read God's Word carefully, to understand clearly, and to apply prayerfully. This study helps us hear James' call to true faith in Jesus Christ—a faith that works. With simple clarity, Keri guides us not only in studying James but also in learning to study the Bible."

Kathleen Nielson is author of the *Living Word Bible Studies*; Director of Women's Initiatives, The Gospel Coalition; and wife of Niel, who served as President of Covenant College from 2002 to 2012.

"It is hard to imagine a better inductive Bible study tool than this one. So many study tools wander from the biblical text, but Keri Folmar's study on James concentrates on what James himself says. Also, the message of James for our everyday lives is constantly emphasized. I recommend this book for both individual and group study, for it will enable you to grow in your faith."

Diane Schreiner, wife of professor, author, and pastor Tom Schreiner and mother of four grown children, has led women's Bible studies for more than 20 years.

"This study through the Book of James encourages us to have an active faith that works itself out in love. I appreciate the way Keri consistently challenges us to apply God's Word to our own hearts, and also to our relationships in the body of Christ. This is a great study to do on your own or in partnership with someone who is not yet a Christian, or with someone who struggles with assurance or expresses a desire to have a vibrant life of faith and service to Christ."

Kristie Anyabwile holds a history degree from NC State University. Her husband, Thabiti, serves as Senior Pastor of First Baptist Church, Grand Cayman, and as a Council Member for The Gospel Coalition.

"What a harvest of righteousness is enjoyed by those who dig deep into the book of James! We all need the wisdom that comes down from above, and this Bible study on James is a true guide. Keri skillfully created this rich resource—and not only that, she put the tools in your hands so you can study God's word for yourself. Gather your friends to study with you, and enjoy the harvest together!"

Gloria Furman is a pastor's wife in the Middle East and author of *Glimpses of Grace* and *Treasuring Christ When Your Hands Are Full.*

Table of Contents

More Bible studies for women from Keri Folmar

Grace: A Bible Study on Ephesians for Women
Joy!—A Bible Study on Philippians for Women

All of Keri's studies are available:

- In bulk discount pricing for as few as 8 copies
- In printable PDF format for $5.45
- Through our ebook licensing program (4 pricing levels)

Learn more at:

bit.ly/JoyStudy
bit.ly/GraceStudy

(See the back pages of this book for more great titles from Cruciform Press.)

Faith: A Bible Study on James for Women | Print / PDF ISBN: 978-1-936760-85-5
Cover Photo: Ruth Elizabeth Folmar

A s we begin this study of James' letter, we should think through why we are studying the Bible. Why not read some other book? Or why not just get together with some other ladies and chat?

Well, have you heard the story about the kindergarten teacher who had her class paint pictures of anything they chose? One little girl was working very intently on her painting. After observing the girl for a moment, the teacher asked, "What are you painting?" The girl answered, "It's a picture of God." Amused, the teacher informed her, "No one knows what God looks like." Without looking up from her painting, the little girl responded, "They will in a minute!"

This might be a cute example of a precocious child, but many people paint pictures in their own minds of how God looks and acts. They "know" God to be a certain way because they want him to be that way.

However, the one true God is transcendent. He is beyond our capacity to know. First Timothy 6:16 describes God, "Who alone has immortality, who dwells in unapproachable light, whom no one has ever seen or can see." God existed before time. He is the creator, and we are his creatures. He cannot be approached by sinful man.

How can we know this God if we cannot approach him? He has to approach us. The only way to truly know God is for him to reveal himself to us. He reveals his existence and power in creation. (See Psalm 19 and Romans 1:18-21.) However, if we want to truly know this God of surpassing worth in a personal way, it must be through his Word.

And God *wants* us, his creatures, to know him. Jeremiah 9:23-24 says:

> Thus says the Lord: "Let not the wise man boast in his wisdom, let not the mighty man boast in his might, let not the rich man boast in his riches, but let him who boasts boast in this, that he understands and knows me, that I am the Lord who practices steadfast love, justice, and righteousness in the earth."

Do you boast in understanding and knowing the Lord? Do you want to know this God who practices love, justice, and righteousness in the earth? He wants you to understand and know him. He is ready to speak to you every morning when you wake up, throughout the day, and before you go to bed. You have only to open his Word.

A well-known catechism says, "The chief end of man is to glorify God and enjoy him forever." That is what we were created for—to truly know and enjoy the God of the universe. Jeremiah the prophet cried out: "Your words were found, and I ate them, and your words became to me a joy and the delight of my heart" (Jeremiah 15:16).

A great saint, C.H. Spurgeon, said:

> Believer! There is enough in the Bible for thee to live upon forever. If thou shouldst outnumber the years of Methuselah, there would be no need for a fresh revelation; if thou shouldst live until Christ should come upon the earth, there would be no necessity for the addition of a single word; if thou shouldst go down as deep as Jonah, or even descend as David said he did, into the depths of hell, still there would be enough in the Bible to comfort thee without a supplementary sentence. (http://spurgeon.org/sermons/0005.htm)

This is why we study the Bible: it is God's revelation of himself to us. We need to know who God truly is and guard against painting our own picture of him. God has revealed himself to us, not in paintings, but through his Son by the words of Scripture. God the creator has spoken, and we his creation should listen to his words as life-sustaining truth and joyfully obey them.

This Bible study workbook is to assist you in studying James' letter in an inductive way. Inductive study is reading the passage in context and asking questions of the text with the purpose of deriving the meaning and significance from the text itself. We really do this automatically every day when we read. When we study the Bible inductively we are after the author's original intent, i.e., what the author meant when he wrote the passage. In this workbook you will figure out the meaning by answering a series of questions about the text, paying close attention to the words and context of the passage.

The theme of James' letter is possessing real faith or having a faith that works. Saturate your study in prayer that your life would be changed as you are challenged, exhorted, and encouraged by James to show your faith by your works.

How to Do Inductive Bible Study

Step 1 – Begin with prayer. "Open my eyes, that I may behold wondrous things out of your law" (Psalm 119:18).

Step 2 – Read the text.

Step 3 – Observation. *The goal of this step is to figure out what the text is saying.* This is where you ask questions like: Who? When? Where? What? These questions should be answered from the very words of the text. Ask yourself if this passage reminds you of any other passages in Scripture. Write down any questions that arise in your mind.

Step 4 – Interpretation. *The goal of this step is to figure out what the text meant to the original hearers.* This most important step is often skipped, but a lack of correct interpretation leads to incorrect application. We cannot understand what God is saying to us if we don't first understand what he was saying to his original audience and why he was saying it.

Your job in interpretation is to figure out the main point of the passage and understand the arguments that support the main point. Your interpretation should flow out of your observations, so keep asking yourself, "Can I support this interpretation based on my observations?"

Here are some questions to ask yourself as you study:

- How does the surrounding context of the passage shed light on its meaning?
- Why did the author include this particular passage in his book?
- Do other passages of Scripture fill out my interpretation?

- Is my interpretation consistent with my overall observations, or is it too dependent on a few details?
- How does this passage fit within the Bible's teaching as a whole? (The context of any passage is ultimately the Bible as a whole.)
- What is the main point of the passage?
- Can I summarize the passage in a few sentences?
- If an Old Testament passage: how does this passage relate to Christ and his work on the cross?

Step 5 – Application. *Prayerfully apply the passage to your own life.* The application should flow from the main point of the text.

Here are some questions to ask yourself in order to apply the text:

- Did I learn something new about God, his ways, his character, his plans, and his priorities? If so, how should I be living in light of this truth?
- Do I need to change my beliefs based on this passage, or is a truth reinforced?
- Is there a behavior I need to adopt or stop?
- Does this passage have implications for the way I should relate to the church?
- Does this passage have implications for the way I relate to or speak to my non-Christian friends?
- How should I pray based on this passage?
- Should I be praising God for something in this passage?
- Do I see a sin for which I need to repent?
- Is there an encouragement or promise on which I need to dwell?

In Summary

Luke 24:44–47 says,

> Then [Jesus] said to them, "These are my words that I spoke to you while I was still with you, that everything written about me in the Law of Moses and the Prophets and the Psalms must be fulfilled." Then he opened their minds to understand the Scriptures, and said to them, "Thus it is written, that the Christ should suffer and on the third day rise from the dead, and that repentance and forgiveness of sins should be proclaimed in his name to all nations, beginning from Jerusalem."

This is why we study the Bible: so that we can know Christ, repent, be forgiven, and proclaim him to the nations. We must keep Jesus in mind when we study Scripture. Adrienne Lawrence writes, "God has one overarching redemptive plan—to glorify himself by creating and redeeming a people for himself through Christ. Christ is at the center of God's plan. All of Scripture in some way speaks to that plan. Keep this in mind as you are doing your study of Scripture."

[Note: This "How to" has been adapted from Adrienne Lawrence's pamphlet on Inductive Bible Study.]

Notes

The first day of this inductive study will be an overview of James. On the following days you will study smaller segments of the letter and answer observation, interpretation, and application questions. The questions were written based on language from the English Standard Version of the Bible. However, you are welcome to use any reliable translation to do the study.

To assist you in recognizing the different types of questions asked, the questions are set out with icons as indicated below.

👁 **Observation:**		Look closely in order to figure out what the text is saying. Get answers directly from the text, using the words of Scripture.
✟ **Interpretation:**		What's the "true north" for this verse? Figure out what the text meant to the original hearers by determining the author's intended meaning.
♥ **Application:**		Apply the passage to your own heart and life, concentrating on the author's intended meaning that you have already determined.

Because Scripture interprets Scripture, many of the questions cite passages in addition to the one you are studying in James. If the question says, "Read…" you will need to read the additional verses cited to answer the question. If the question says, "See…" the verses help you answer the question but are not necessary. "See also…" signals you to read the verses if you would like to study the answer to the question further.

You only need your Bible to do this study of James, and in fact I highly recommend first answering the questions directly from your Bible before looking at any other materials. That said, it may be helpful for you to confirm your answers, especially if you are leading others in a group study. To check your answers or for further study, *The Message of James*, by J. Alec Motyer, is excellent. For helpful overviews of the passages, Kent Hughes has published a series of sermons called, *James: Faith That Works*.

For more general help in knowing how to study the Bible, I

highly recommend *Bible Study: Following the Ways of the Word*, by Kathleen Buswell Nielson and *Dig Deeper! Tools to Unearth the Bible's Treasure*, by Nigel Beynon and Andrew Sach. Bible study teachers and students who want a closer look at New Testament theology that will also encourage your heart can read Thomas Schreiner's, *Magnifying God in Christ: A Summary of New Testament Theology*.

Notes for Leaders

This Bible study can be done by individuals alone, but the best context for Bible study is the local church. When small groups of women gather together to study the Scriptures, it promotes unity and ignites spiritual growth within the church.

The study was designed for ladies to complete five days of "homework" and then come together to discuss their answers in a small group. The goal of gathering in small groups is to promote discussion among ladies to sharpen one another by making sure all understand the meaning of the text and can apply it to their lives. As ladies discuss, their eyes may be opened to applications of the text they didn't see while doing the individual study. Believers will encourage one another in their knowledge of the gospel, and unbelievers will hear the gospel clearly explained. As a result, ladies will learn from one another and come away from group Bible study with a deeper understanding of the text and a better knowledge of how to read the Bible on their own in their private times of study and prayer.

If you are leading a small group, you will have some extra homework to do. First, know what Bible study is and is not. Bible study is not primarily a place to meet felt needs, eat good food and chat, receive counseling, or have a free-for-all discussion. All of these things tend to happen in a ladies' Bible study, but they should not take over the focus. Bible study is digging into the Scriptures to get the true meaning of the text and applying it to lives that change as a result.

Second, make sure you know the main points of the text before leading discussion by carefully studying the passage and checking yourself using a good commentary, like one of those listed above. You may also find a Bible dictionary and concordance helpful. Second Timothy 3:16-17 says, "All Scripture is breathed out by God and profitable for teaching, for reproof, for correction, and for training in righteousness, that the man [or woman] of God may be complete, equipped for every good work." Scripture is powerful. That power comes through truth. Scripture is not like a magical incantation where you mouth some words and see the effect. Instead, we must know what the text of Scripture means before we apply it and see its work of transformation in our lives. Your job as a discussion leader is not to directly teach, nor to simply facilitate discussion, but rather to lead ladies in finding the meaning of the text and help them see how it is "profitable" and can make them "complete, equipped for every good work."

Third, pray. Pray for the ladies in your group during the week while you prepare. Pray as you start your small group study, asking the Holy Spirit to illuminate the Scripture to your minds and apply it to your hearts. And encourage ladies to pray based on what they studied at the end of your small group time. Ask the Holy Spirit to use his sword, the Word of God, in the lives of your ladies.

Fourth, draw ladies out and keep your discussion organized. Choose what you determine are the most important questions from the study guide, focusing the bulk of your discussion on the interpretation and application questions. Ask a question, but don't answer it! Be comfortable with long pauses, or rephrase questions you think the group didn't understand. Not answering the questions yourself may be a bit awkward at first, but it will promote discussion in the end because your ladies will know they have to do the answering. Feel free to affirm good answers or sum up after ladies have had time to discuss. This gives clarity to the discussion. However, don't feel the need to fill in every detail and nuance you gleaned from your personal study. Your goal is to get your group talking.

Fifth, keep your focus on the Scriptures. The Holy Spirit uses God's Word to change ladies' hearts. Don't be afraid of wrong answers. Gently use them to clarify and teach by directing attention back to the Scriptures for the right answers. If ladies go off on unhelpful tangents, direct them back to the question and address the tangent later one on one or with reading material. However, if the tangent is on a vital question that goes to the gospel, take time to talk about it. These are God-given opportunities.

Sixth, be sure you focus on the gospel. In your prep time, ask yourself what the text has to do with the gospel and look for opportunities to ask questions to bring out the gospel. Hopefully, your church members will invite unbelievers to your study who will hear the glorious good news. But even if your group is made up of all believers, we never get beyond our need to be reminded of Christ crucified and what that means for our lives.

Lastly, enjoy studying the Scriptures with your ladies. Your love and passion for the Word of God will be contagious, and you will have the great joy of watching your ladies catch it and rejoice in the Word with you.

James' Letter to the Twelve Tribes in the Dispersion

James was the half-brother of Jesus and a pillar of the Jerusalem church. He became known as James the Just for his faithfulness to the law, love for the saints, and constancy in prayer. James wrote his letter, most likely sometime in the mid to late 40s and, according to tradition, was killed by scribes and Pharisees for his refusal to denounce Christ in 62 A.D.

James' letter is written with a pastor's heart. The Jerusalem church was dispersed after the stoning of Stephen, and they scattered as far as Phoenicia, Cyprus, and Antioch. They were Jewish believers living in the Gentile world, trying to rebuild their lives in the midst of temptation, difficulty, and persecution.

James is a book about having true faith—a faith that works. It is from a pastor to his beloved brothers and sisters, urging them to live out their faith, even while the world, the devil, and their own flesh give them much trouble. James is an eminently practical letter to encourage us to live out our faith in the God who sent his Son, Jesus, to die that we might be brought forth to truly live for him.

And this I do boldly and confidently say, that true holiness is a great reality. It is something in a man that can be seen, and known, and marked, and felt by all around him. It is light: if it exists, it will show itself. It is salt: if it exists, its savour will be perceived. It is a precious ointment: if it exists, its presence cannot be hid.

—J.C. Ryle, *Holiness: Its Nature, Hindrances, Difficulties & Roots* (Moscow, ID: Charles Nolan Publishers, 2001) p 47

Begin your study each day praying for the Lord to give you wisdom to understand the purpose for trials in our lives so you can rejoice in what he will do in and through them.

Pray.

Read through James 1-5.

Write down any themes or observations that stand out to you.

Are any subjects repeated?

Is there an overall tone to the book of James?

Jot down any questions you have at this initial reading.

Remember:

◉ **Observation:** Figure out what the text is saying. Get the answer from the words of Scripture.

✛ **Interpretation:** Figure out the meaning of the text. What did the writer intend to convey?

♥ **Application:** Prayerfully apply the passage to your own life. The application should flow from the main point of the text.

Pray.

Read James 1:1.

◉ 1. Who wrote this letter?

◉ 2. How does James describe himself?

◉ 3. Who was James? Read Acts 12:17; 21:18 and Galatians 1:19.

✛ 4. Why do you think James describes himself as a servant of God and of the Lord Jesus Christ instead of as Jesus' brother and an apostle who is the leader of the church in Jerusalem?

✛ 5. What lesson can we learn from James' humility as we relate to each other in the church?

👁 6. To whom is James writing his letter?

✦ 7. Who are the twelve tribes?

✦ 8. What does the "Dispersion" refer to? See Acts 8:1 and 11:19.

✦ 9. In your own words, who do you think James' letter was
     written for?

✦ 10. What would people who are dispersed be going through?

✦ 11. Does James' letter apply to non-Jewish Christians today? See
      Galatians 3:28-29.

♥ 12. Think about your life. In what ways do you feel like a part of a people who have been dispersed?

♥ 13. Read Jeremiah 31:10-14 and Revelation 21:22-27. How do these passages give you hope as you begin your study of James?

Day 3

Pray.

Read James 1:2-4.

👁 1. What does James call the people to whom he is writing?

✦ 2. What makes one a brother or sister of James?

👁 3. How does James tell his readers to respond to trials?

👁 4. What kind of trials should believers respond to with joy?

✦ 5. List some of the various kinds of trials a believer may meet with.

◉ 6. What is God's purpose for trials in the believer's life?

✦ 7. What does it mean that God tests your faith through these trials?

◉ 8. What do trials produce in a believer's life?

✦ 9. What is steadfastness?

◉ 10. What is the effect of steadfastness?

✦ 11. What does Christ's death and resurrection have to do with having joy in trials?

✦ 12. Putting this together, why should believers respond to trials with joy?

♥ 13. What are some trials you are currently undergoing?

♥ 14. How can you have joy in the midst of these trials?

Pray.

Read James 1:2-8.

James 1:5-8

◉ 1. What does James tell believers to do if they lack wisdom?

◉ 2. What will God give to the believers who ask for wisdom, and how will God give it?

✦ 3. What does this tell you about God?

✦ 4. What is wisdom from God? (What does asking for wisdom have to do with previous verses?)

◉ 5. How is the believer to ask for wisdom?

◉ 6. What is the doubting person like?

✦ 7. What does it mean for a person to be like a wave of the sea?

👁 8. What should the man who doubts expect from the Lord?

👁 9. What is the man who doubts (see v 8)?

✦ 10. What does it mean for the doubter to be double-minded and unstable?

✦ 11. How is this section of Scripture related to what you studied yesterday in verses 2-4?

✦ 12. Putting all this together, what does it mean to ask for wisdom in faith without doubting?

♥ 13. Look back at the trials you listed yesterday. Do you believe God is in control even of these difficulties in your life? Do you believe he has sent them into your life for his good purposes? If so, then pray about these things asking God for his wisdom in them and for joy through them.

Day 5

Pray.

Read James 1:2-11.

James 1:9-11

👁 1. What are the two types of brothers James addresses in verses 9 and 10?

👁 2. What is the lowly brother to boast in?

✛ 3. In what way has the lowly brother been exalted? See Galatians 3:28-29. Can you back up your answer with any other passages in the Bible?

👁 4. What is the rich brother to boast in?

✦ 5. What does verse 11 have to do with the rich man boasting in his humiliation?

✦ 6. What does it mean for the rich man to boast in his humiliation? See Philippians 3:2-11.

✦ 7. What does James intend for both poor and rich believers to boast in? See Galatians 6:14.

❤ 8. In what way can you boast in your:

Exaltation in Christ	Humiliation in Christ

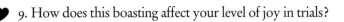 9. How does this boasting affect your level of joy in trials?

End this week praying that it would bring you great joy to boast only in Christ in every circumstance.

Begin your time of study each day praying for the Lord to give you steadfast faith in him in the midst of any trial.

Read James 1:1-11.

✦ 1. How would you sum up the meaning of the following verses you studied last week?

   ✦ Verses 2-4:

   ✦ Verses 5-8:

   ✦ Verses 9-11:

♥ 2. Using these verses, draw up a mental plan of attack to deal with difficult circumstances that come into your life.

   ♥ Verses 2-4:

♥ Verses 5-8:

♥ Verses 9-11:

Day 2

Read James 1:2-18.

James 1:12

👁 1. What is the man (or woman) who remains steadfast under trial?

👁 2. How is that woman blessed?

✦ 3. What does it mean to remain steadfast under trial?

👁 4. When will the blessed woman receive the crown of life?

✦ 5. When will it be shown that she has stood the test? See also
Revelation 2:9-11 and 1 Peter 5:4.

✦ 6. What does it mean to stand the test?

Note: In verse 12, James is saying that perseverance (passing
the test) is a pre-condition for obtaining the crown of life.
If you fail the test you don't get the crown. Is this works-
righteousness? No! James (like other New Testament writers)
is clear that salvation is ultimately an act of God's sovereign
grace alone (See 1:18, 21; Ephesians 2:8-9; 1 Peter 1:3, 23).
However, the person who has been truly transformed (brought
forth) by God will invariably live a new life animated by the
Holy Spirit. Thus, God enables his people to persevere to the
end. If they don't persevere, they never were truly his. (See 1
Corinthians 15:2, Philippians 1:6, Colossians 1:23, Jude 24-25,
and Revelation 2:10-11.)

✦ 7. In what sense are difficult circumstances in our lives like tests?
See Romans 5:3-4.

✦ 8. What is the crown of life? Read 1 Corinthians 9:24-27 and 2 Timothy 4:8.

👁 9. To whom has God promised the crown of life in James 1:12?

♥ 10. Remember the trials you listed in Week 1, Day 3. What would it look like for you to remain steadfast in these trials?

♥ 11. How can verse 12 both motivate and comfort you when you go through trials?

♥ 12. How can you use this verse to add to your plan of attack from Day 1?

Day 3
Read James 1:2-18.

James 1:13-15

👁 1. What should one not say?

👁 2. Can God be tempted to do evil?

👁 3. Does God tempt anyone to do evil?

👁 4. Where does temptation come from?

👁 5. Describe the progression from desire to death.

✛ 6. What is the difference between James saying that God tests (v 12) and someone accusing God of tempting them?

✛ 7. How does one remain steadfast under trial as opposed to giving in to sin?

❤ 8. If God ordains the difficult circumstances in your life for your good, how do you think he wants you to respond to them?

✦ 9. Does God ordain or plan even the acts that people intend for evil? Read Exodus 7:3-5, Proverbs 16:4, Ephesians 1:11, and 2 Thessalonians 2:11-12.

✦ 10. How do you explain how God can ordain acts that are evil, but does not tempt anyone to evil, and is therefore not responsible for their evil? Read Genesis 50:19-20, regarding Joseph's brothers selling him into slavery, and Acts 4:27-28, regarding the crucifixion of Jesus. (Hint: What is God's purpose in all things, as opposed to the evil-doer's purpose for the act?)

Day 4

Read James 1:12-18.

James 1:16-17

👁 1. What does James tell his beloved brothers not to be?

👁 2. Where does every good and perfect gift come from?

👁 3. How is God the Father described?

✦ 4. What are some good and perfect gifts from the Father? See Luke 11:13.

✦ 5. What do these good and perfect gifts have to do with the previous verses you've studied?

✦ 6. What does God being the "Father of lights with whom there is no variation or shadow due to change" mean?

✦ 7. Why do you think James reminds his readers that God is good and does not change?

✦ 8. Going back to the beginning of this section, what do you think James' readers can be deceived about?

✦ 9. What do these reminders about God's character have to do with trials?

♥ 10. When you are struggling through trials, do you ever doubt God's continuing goodness toward you? How does remembering God's character help you when you are facing difficulty?

Day 5

Read James 1:16-18.

James 1:18

👁 1. Whose will is James writing about?

👁 2. What has God done by his will?

👁 3. Whom has God brought forth?

✦ 4. Read John 3:3-8 and 1 Peter 1:23.

   ✦ a) What does it mean to be brought forth?

   👁 b) By what means does God bring people forth?

✦ 5. What is the Word of truth? Read Ephesians 1:13.

✦ 6. Who is acting in verse 18, and who therefore does the work of salvation? See also Acts 11:18 and Ephesians 2:8-9.

✦ 7. What does the word *that* in verse 18 tell us?

👁 8. What should the person who is brought forth by God be?

✦ 9. Firstfruits refers to an Old Testament regulation requiring farmers to set apart the first of their crop for the Lord. J.A. Motyer makes three points about this offering:

i) Out of all that belonged to the Lord, this was *specially* his; the rest remained to be used in the ordinary purposes of life; ii) the first-fruits had to be the best, and were set apart as holy to the Lord; iii) the offering of the first-fruits was an annual reminder that the Lord keeps his promises to his people, bringing them from slavery, giving them a homeland, providing for them in it. (J.A. Motyer, *The Message of James* [Inter-Varsity Press, 1985])

✦ What is James telling his readers God's purpose for the church is?

✦ 10. What does God calling people forth to be dedicated to him have to do with trials?

♥ 11. If God has called you forth by his will, opening your eyes and causing you to believe the gospel, what should your response be?

♥ 12. In what way could someone looking at your life tell that you are dedicated to the Lord?

♥ 13. In what areas of life can you increase your dedication to the Lord?

♥ Personal devotion:

♥ Time or money:

♥ Family:

♥ Encouraging the saints:

♥ Work:

♥ Dealing with difficult circumstances:

End this week by praying that you would be wholly dedicated to the Lord and that you would be steadfast under trial to stand the test so that you will receive the crown of life.

Begin your study each day praying that you would be a doer of the word, not just a hearer.

Read James 1:19-27.

✦ 1. After reading this section, what do you think is happening in the churches?

◉ 2. James is about to write some commands that convict the hearts of his readers. How does James describe the brothers (and sisters) to whom he is writing?

✦ 3. By whom are these believers beloved, and why do you think James is reminding them of this?

◉ 4. What does James want his readers to know?

Discuss the meaning of the phrases below and the importance of obeying these commands:

	Meaning	Importance
✦ 5. Quick to hear		
✦ 6. Slow to speak		
✦ 7. Slow to anger		

👁 8. What does anger not produce?

✦ 9. What does verse 20 mean in your own words?

✦ 10. How could one mistakenly use anger to try to produce righteousness?

✦ 11. How do being quick to hear, slow to speak, and slow to anger work together to reduce strife and build good relationships?

✦ 12. Why is this so important in a church in which different ages, cultures, and types of people come together as one family?

♥ 13. Which of these qualities (or combination of all three) do you need to work on?

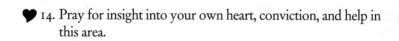 14. Pray for insight into your own heart, conviction, and help in this area.

Day 2

Read James 1:19-27.

James 1:21

👁 1. What does James tell the beloved brothers to put away?

👁 2. How much of it are they to put away?

👁 3. What does James tell the beloved brothers to receive?

✦ 4. What is the implanted word?

👁 5. How are they to receive the word?

✦ 6. Why is meekness needed to receive the word?

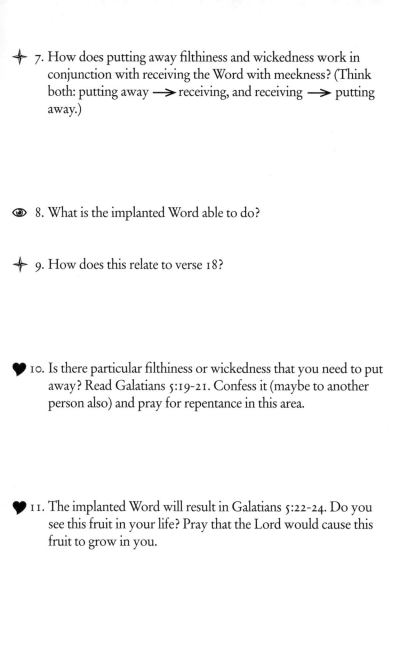

✦ 7. How does putting away filthiness and wickedness work in conjunction with receiving the Word with meekness? (Think both: putting away ⟶ receiving, and receiving ⟶ putting away.)

👁 8. What is the implanted Word able to do?

✦ 9. How does this relate to verse 18?

♥ 10. Is there particular filthiness or wickedness that you need to put away? Read Galatians 5:19-21. Confess it (maybe to another person also) and pray for repentance in this area.

♥ 11. The implanted Word will result in Galatians 5:22-24. Do you see this fruit in your life? Pray that the Lord would cause this fruit to grow in you.

Read James 1:19-27.

James 1:22-25

1. What does James tell his readers to be?

2. What does James tell his readers not to only be?

3. What is the word?

4. What do those who hear the Word and don't do it, do to themselves?

5. What is the simile James uses for the man who hears the Word and doesn't do it?

6. In your own words how would you describe the danger of hearing the Word and not doing it?

7. In contrast, who will be blessed, and in what will he be blessed?

✦ 8. What does it mean for him to be blessed in his doing?

✦ 9. What is the perfect law, the law of liberty?

✦ 10. What do persevering and doing have to do with one another?

✦ 11. How are these verses connected to the previous paragraph?

✦ 12. Notice, one must be a hearer of the Word before we can be doers. In what ways do we hear the Word?

❤ 13. In what ways can you increase your hearing of the Word?

♥ 14. Can you think of specific times in your own life when you have been a hearer and doer of the word? Describe one of those times.

♥ 15. In what ways can you make sure that you are not like the man looking in the mirror and forgetting, but like the doer who acts?

♥ 16. Jesus said,

> Why do you call me "Lord, Lord," and not do what I tell you? Everyone who comes to me and hears my words and does them, I will show you what he is like: he is like a man building a house, who dug deep and laid the foundation on the rock. And when a flood arose, the stream broke against that house and could not shake it, because it had been well built. But the one who hears and does not do them is like a man who built a house on the ground without a foundation. When the stream broke against it, immediately it fell, and the ruin of that house was great (Luke 6:46-49).

Is there anything specific you have heard from the Word that you need to do?

Read James 1:19-27.

✦ 1. Summarize James' command from verses 22-25 that you studied yesterday.

James 1:26

👁 2. What type of person does James address in verse 26?

✦ 3. What does it mean to be religious?

👁 4. What makes a person's religion worthless?

✦ 5. A bridle is used by a rider to control a horse. What does it mean to bridle the tongue, and what does it look like when one doesn't bridle the tongue?

✦ 6. How can one deceive her own heart, and what does that have to do with the tongue?

✦ 7. How is this verse on the tongue connected to previous verses like 19 and following?

♥ 8. In what ways do you need to bridle your tongue? Consider Ephesians 4:29-32.

Day 5

Read James 1:19-27.

James 1:27

1. What acts show that one's religion is pure and undefiled before God?

2. How were orphans and widows treated at the time James wrote this letter?

3. In what ways do you (or can you) reach out to those who are needy and can give you nothing in return?

4. What does it mean to be stained by the world?

5. In what ways can the world stain us?

6. How can we keep ourselves unstained from the world? (Remember v 21.)

♥ 7. Are you listening more to the Word of God or to the world? How can you increase input from God and decrease input from the world in your life? (Also, if you have children, consider these same questions for them.)

Notes

Begin your study each morning by praying that you would not show partiality in the church. Pray for the Lord to expand your friendships to include people of differing nationalities, economic status, ages, and stages of life.

Read James 1:19-2:26.

✦ 1. How would you summarize the verses, James 1:19-27, from your study last week?

✦ 2. What is the tone of James chapter 2?

✦ 3. From reading chapter 2, what are some of the issues the churches are struggling with that James is writing to address?

Read James 2:1-13.

James 2:1-4

👁 1. Answer the folowing:

    👁 a) What is James' command to the brothers?

    👁 b) What is the basis for this command?

👁 2. What is the example of showing partiality?

👁 3. If one makes distinctions like this, what has one become?

✦ 4. What does it mean to be a judge with evil thoughts in this context?

♥ 5. Do you make distinctions in the church? How many friends from different ethnic groups do you have? How many friends of different ages or in differing stages of life do you have? Do you show hospitality to those who cannot return it? Whom do you greet at church?

Read James 1:26-2:13.

James 2:5-7

👁 1. Whom has God chosen, and for what purpose?

👁 2. To whom has God promised the kingdom?

👁 3. Why is James writing to these Christians about showing partiality?

👁 4. Why does it not make sense for them to show partiality to the rich?

✛ 5. What does it mean to be poor in the world? See Matthew 5:3.

✛ 6. How does one become rich in faith? See 2 Corinthians 8:9.

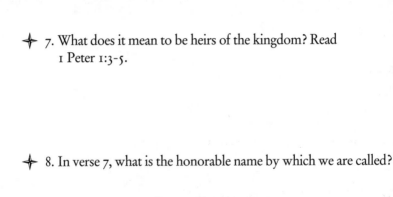

✦ 7. What does it mean to be heirs of the kingdom? Read 1 Peter 1:3-5.

✦ 8. In verse 7, what is the honorable name by which we are called?

✦ 9. How are these verses related to James 1:9?

✦ 10. What is the difference between what the world values and what God values?

♥ 11. Most of us belong to churches with people from diverse socioeconomic groups. Can you see ways in which you struggle with the sin of partiality in your church?

♥ 12. What are some ways you have had or have seen positive interactions between diverse peoples in your church?

♥ 13. Have you given up your trust in the riches of the world to be called by his honorable name? If not, consider the difference between the passing riches of this world and the eternal inheritance that comes with being a child of God. Ask God to give you eyes that see all Christians as children of God who will be co-inheritors with you in his kingdom, and rejoice as we wait together until that day.

Day 4

Read James 2:1-13.

James 2:8-13

👁 1. What is the royal law according to the Scripture?

✢ 2. What is the contrast that James sets up in verses 8 and 9?

◉ 3. Why is one who shows partiality a transgressor?

✦ 4. Explain why failing in one point of the law makes one accountable for all of it.

◉ 5. What is the remedy for this?

✦ 6. Read Galatians 3:10-14. What is the law of liberty?

✦ 7. How does one speak and act as judged under the law of liberty?

◉ 8. What will be given to the one who has shown no mercy? See also Matthew 5:7.

◉ 9. What triumphs over judgment?

✦ 10. What does showing mercy have to do with not being partial to the rich?

♥ 11. Look in your heart. Are there ways you judge others who are different from you?

♥ 12. In his book, *Humility*, C.J. Mahaney recommends actively looking for evidences of grace in other church members' lives. He says,

"Look anywhere and you'll see evidences of God's activity, evidences of grace. What a joy and a privilege it is to discern this activity in the lives of those we love and care for—and to draw their attention to how God is at work in their lives." (C.J. Mahaney, *Humility* [Sisters, OR: Multnomah Books, 2005] p 101)

Pray that instead of seeing how others are different, you would see evidence of grace in others' lives.

Read 1 Corinthians 1:26-31.

✦ 1. Summarize what God has chosen to do in 1 Corinthians 1:26-28.

👁 2. What is God's reason for doing it this way according to verse 29?

👁 3. Who is the cause of our life in Christ?

👁 4. How does verse 30 describe Jesus?

✦ 5. Can we take any credit for our wisdom, righteousness, sanctification or redemption? Explain.

👁 6. What should we, who have been given life in Christ, boast in?

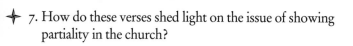 7. How do these verses shed light on the issue of showing partiality in the church?

8. What are some ways you can reach out more to brothers and sisters in the church who are different from you?

End this week praying for your church that you would not show partiality.

Begin your times of study this week praying for true faith that is shown by your works.

Read James 2:14-26.

James 2:14-17

✦ 1. Summarize James' first two rhetorical questions in verse 14.

✦ 2. What are the implied answers to these questions?

👁 3. What kind of faith is James concerned with?

✦ 4. What does James' example of verbally blessing someone without taking care of their physical needs illustrate? Why do you think James uses this example?

👁 5. What does James mean by faith without works?

✦ 6. What does it mean for faith without works to be dead?

✦ 7. Do you think this section of James' letter is connected to the previous section? If so, how are they connected? (What works of faith does James seem to be most concerned about in the church?)

♥ 8. Second Corinthians 13:5 says, "Examine yourselves, to see whether you are in the faith." How does James' discussion on faith and works help us examine ourselves?

♥ 9. What evidence do you see in your life that your faith is alive?

♥ 10. Give praise to God for the evidence you see. See Ephesians 2:10 and Philippians 2:13.

♥ 11. If you don't see much evidence, consider that you may believe in your head but not have true faith in Jesus that results in good works. Read and meditate on 1 John 1:5-9. Verse 9 tells us that God is faithful and just to forgive our sins and to cleanse us from all unrighteousness if we confess our sins. God created us to live for him, but we have all turned away from him and lived for ourselves. Romans 6:23 says that the wages of sin — turning away from God and living for ourselves — is death. But verse 23 continues, "the free gift of God is eternal life in Christ Jesus our Lord." God sent his Son, Jesus, to pay our wages for us. He died on the cross, taking God's wrath — the punishment for our sins — and rose from the dead, showing he had conquered sin and death. You can have this free gift of eternal life in Christ by confessing your sins and putting your trust in Christ's finished work on the cross. The result will be, not a perfect life, but a transformed life characterized by faith that works.

Day 2

Read James 2:14-26.

James 2:18-25

👁 1. Review verse 14. With what kind of faith is James concerned?

👁 2. What argument does James anticipate in verse 18?

✦ 3. Explain this argument in your own words.

◉ 4. What does James say to this argument?

◉ 5. James uses three examples (one negative and two positive) to illustrate showing faith by works. What are they?

   ◉ a.

   ◉ b.

   ◉ c.

Let's take the next few days to unpack each of these illustrations. The first is a negative example. Today we'll examine the "faith" of demons.

◉ 6. What do the demons believe?

✦ 7. From Mark 1:23-24 and Acts 16:16-17, what else do demons seem to understand?

⊚ 8. What reaction does this knowledge cause in them? See also Luke 8:26-31.

✦ 9. Are demons exercising saving faith when they believe that there is one God (and even that Jesus is his Son)? Why not?

♥ 10. Can you think of ways that people who call themselves Christians rely on "faith" that is separated from works?

⊚ 11. What does James call this type of person in verse 20, and what will he show him?

✦ 12. Why is it foolish for a person to argue that because she is saved by faith, it does not matter how she lives?

Day 3

Read James 2:14-26.

James 2:21-23

👁 1. What illustration does James use in verses 21-23?

👁 2. Read Genesis 22:1-18 for the harrowing story of Abraham offering up Isaac. God had promised Abraham that he would make him into a great nation through his son Isaac. What does God ask Abraham to do?

👁 3. When does Abraham proceed to do what God asks of him?

👁 4. When Isaac asks his father where the lamb for the offering is, how does Abraham respond?

👁 5. Abraham obeys God, believing that God will fulfill his promise even if Isaac is killed. See Hebrews 11:17-19. What does the angel of the Lord say when he stops Abraham from slaying Isaac?

👁 6. What sacrifice does God provide?

👁 7. The angel of the Lord pronounces great blessing on Abraham. What does he give as his reason for the blessings in Genesis 22:16, 18?

👁 8. How does James describe the relationship between Abraham's faith and works in James 2:22?

✛ 9. James quotes from Genesis 15 (before Abraham offered Isaac) in verse 23. How are Abraham's actions with Isaac a fulfillment of Genesis 15:6?

👁 10. What does verse 23 say was counted to Abraham as righteousness, and what was Abraham called?

✛ 11. Explain how the Scriptures can equate Abraham's offering Isaac with believing God.

✛ 12. Based on Abraham's example, how would you define saving faith?

Day 4

Read James 2:14-26.

James 2:24-25

👁 1. By what is a person justified?

✦ 2. What do you think the word *justified* means here in James? (See also vv 21, 25.)

✦ 3. Summarize the story of Rahab from Joshua 2:1-22 and 6:22-25.

👁 4. What was Rahab?

👁 5. How did Rahab describe God?

✦ 6. What did Rahab risk based on her belief about the God of Israel?

✦ 7. If Rahab had not helped the spies, what would have happened to her and her family?

👁 8. What does James say "justified" Rahab?

✦ 9. How does Rahab the prostitute illustrate faith? See also Hebrews 11:31.

✦ 10. How is Rahab an illustration of what happens when a woman embraces the gospel of Jesus Christ? (Note: Rahab, a prostitute from Jericho, was fully embraced by the people of Israel. She married Salmon the father of Boaz, the honorable man who married Ruth, the grandmother of the great King David from whose descendents Jesus was born.)

♥ 11. In what way have you experienced this transformation of becoming part of the people of God?

♥ 12. Rahab gave up the darkness and pain of her former life and trusted the God of the heavens above and the earth beneath. She was fully embraced by God and his people. If you are not a part of the people of God, what is holding you back?

Read James 2:14-26.

James 2:26

◉ 1. With what does James compare faith without works in verse 26?

◉ 2. What does James mean by faith apart from works?

✝ 3. Verse 24 says, "A person is justified by works and not by faith alone." However, Paul, in Romans 3:28, writes, "For we hold that one is justified by faith apart from works of the law." All Scripture is God-breathed, which means that it ultimately has one author—it is the very Word of God. God cannot contradict himself. How would you explain the consistency of these two verses to a friend?

♥ 4. Looking back at Abraham and Rahab, we see that both of these great saints believed God was worthy of being obeyed and would fulfill his promises. Abraham was willing to give up his beloved son, and Rahab risked her life, because they had faith. What about you? When the going gets tough, do you trust God and obey? Take some time to examine these issues in your life.

♥ Submission:

♥ Anxiety:

♥ Complaining:

♥ Loving others:

♥ Forgiving others:

♥ 5. James brings together saving faith and work. How should this affect the way you share the gospel?

♥ 6. How should it affect the community of your church?

Notes

Begin your study each day praying for a tongue that speaks encouragement and wisdom into others' lives.

Read James 3:1-18.

James 3:1-5a

👁 1. Why should not many become teachers?

👁 2. Who stumbles in many ways?

👁 3. If someone does not stumble in what he says, what is he, and what is he able to do?

✝ 4. What is James illustrating with the bit in a horse's mouth and the rudder of a ship?

👁 5. Of what can the tongue boast even though it is a small part of the body?

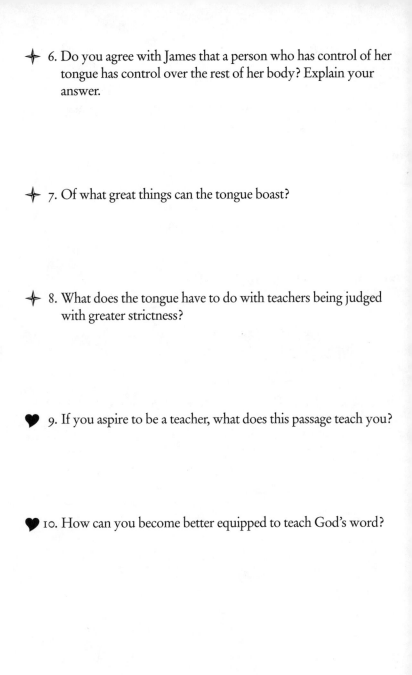

6. Do you agree with James that a person who has control of her tongue has control over the rest of her body? Explain your answer.

7. Of what great things can the tongue boast?

8. What does the tongue have to do with teachers being judged with greater strictness?

9. If you aspire to be a teacher, what does this passage teach you?

10. How can you become better equipped to teach God's word?

♥ 11. What area of your speech do you need to bring under control?

♥ 12. This week try to keep your tongue under control. Keep a mental note of (or you may even want to write these incidents down) when you say something you shouldn't—like gossip, unkind or harsh speech, coarse language, lying, or complaining. Then review it at the end of the week.

Day 2

Read James 3:1-18.

James 3:5b-12

✦ 1. What is the tone of this paragraph?

✦ 2. Why do you think James writes about the tongue with such passion? What might be happening in the church?

◉ 3. What is the first illustration James uses to describe the power of the tongue?

◉ 4. What is the tongue?

◉ 5. What does the tongue set on fire?

◉ 6. Where does the fire come from?

✦ 7. What is James illustrating about the tongue when he refers to animals?

◉ 8. How is the tongue described at the end of verse 8?

♥ 9. Do James' illustrations ring true to you? Can you think of times you have said something you shouldn't have said—when it just "slipped out?" Can you think of times when you should have said something and didn't? Describe some of those times.

◉ 10. What two things does the tongue do?

⊚ 11. What does James say about our tongues blessing God and cursing people?

⊚ 12. Why shouldn't Christians bless God and curse people?

✦ 13. What is James illustrating when he refers to fruit trees and a salt pond?

✦ 14. Read Matthew 12:33-35. Explain James' illustration in light of what Jesus said, "For out of the abundance of the heart the mouth speaks."

♥ 15. Examine your life. In what ways do you "curse" people with your tongue? Unhelpful criticism? Unkind or angry words? Bragging? Gossip? Lying? Try to think of specific people and circumstances.

♥ 16. Pray for the Lord to illuminate these difficult areas of your life and to give you the gift of repentance. "If we confess our sins, he is faithful and just to forgive us our sins and to cleanse us from all unrighteousness" (1 John 1:9).

Day 3

Read James 3:1-12.

Let's look at some verses that go along with James' warnings about the tongue.

Proverbs has much to say on the subject. Put these Proverbs in your own words:

✦ 1. Proverbs 10:8

✦ 2. Proverbs 12:18-19

✦ 3. Proverbs 13:3

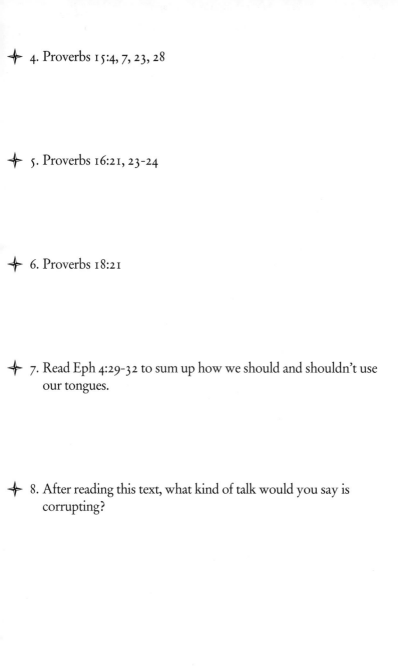

✦ 4. Proverbs 15:4, 7, 23, 28

✦ 5. Proverbs 16:21, 23-24

✦ 6. Proverbs 18:21

✦ 7. Read Eph 4:29-32 to sum up how we should and shouldn't use our tongues.

✦ 8. After reading this text, what kind of talk would you say is corrupting?

Faith

9. What kind of talk is good for building up, giving grace to those who hear? Give specific examples.

10. Can you think of steps you can take to reduce corrupting talk and increase that which builds up?

Day 4

Read James 3:13-18.

1. What does James tell the wise and understanding person to do?

2. What does meekness mean?

3. What is the wisdom from above?

4. How are meekness and wisdom related?

✛ 5. What does it mean to show works in the meekness of wisdom by your good conduct?

👁 6. What does James tell those who have bitter jealousy and selfish ambition in their hearts to do?

👁 7. How does James describe bitter jealousy and selfish ambition?

✛ 8. Why do you think James tells those with jealousy and selfish ambition to not be false about it?

✛ 9. Why do you think James contrasts the meekness of wisdom with jealousy and selfish ambition?

✛ 10. How are these things related to the previous instructions about the tongue?

👁 11. What is the result of jealousy and selfish ambition?

👁 12. What is the result of wisdom from above?

❤ 13. Examine yourself for any jealousy or selfish ambition. What circumstances cause you to be tempted toward these sins?

❤ 14. Considering these circumstances, what would your conduct look like if you replaced the jealousy or selfishness with wisdom from above? Apply one or more of the characteristics of wisdom from above to the situation.

❤ 15. Consider that God sends these trials into your life as a good gift to teach you to respond, not with jealousy or selfish ambition, but with wisdom from above. Give thanks and praise to God for his goodness in using difficult things to make you more like Christ.

Read James 3:1-18.

♥ 1. How did you do this week controlling your tongue? Did you
let any corrupting talk come out of your mouth? Did you say
only what would build others up?

♥ 2. What were some of the consequences of what you said or left
unsaid this week?

♥ 3. Read Matthew 12:33-37. In light of the connection between the
tongue and the heart, how can you work to get your tongue
under control?

James 4:1-12

Week 7

Day 1

Faith in Relationship

Pray this week to see your own heart with regard to quarrels and conflicts that arise, and pray that you would be wholeheartedly devoted to the Lord.

Read James 3:13–4:12.

James 4:1

◉ 1. What is the first question James asks his readers?

✦ 2. Who are the quarrels and fights among?

◉ 3. James answers his first question with another question. What is it?

◉ 4. What does James say is at war within us?

✦ 5. How would you describe the passions that are at war within us? (Is there anything at the end of chapter 3 that ties in here?)

Faith

✦ 6. What should the Christian's greatest passion be?

♥ 7. If our own passions are the cause of fights and quarrels we get into with our brothers and sisters in Christ (and our families), what should we do when a conflict arises?

♥ 8. What are some helpful ways to examine our own hearts when a conflict arises?

♥ 9. Can you think of a quarrel or fight you have had recently with someone in the church or a family member? What passion or desire in your own heart led to or exacerbated this quarrel?

♥ 10. Pray for the Lord to help you make him and his glory your greatest passion and to see when something else competes for God's place in your heart.

Read James 3:13-4:6a.

James 4:2-5

👁 1. What is causing James' readers to murder?

👁 2. What is causing James' readers to fight and quarrel?

✝ 3. Read Matthew 5:21-26, and summarize Jesus' teaching.

✝ 4. Do you think that people in the church James is writing to are actually being killed by one another? How would you describe what is going on among these believers? (Refer back to your summary of Matthew 5:21-26.)

👁 5. Why do these believers not "have"?

👁 6. Why do they not receive when they do ask God for something?

👁 7. What does James call his readers, and why?

8. What does James equate with friendship with the world?

9. What does it mean to be a friend of the world?

10. What does enmity with God mean?

11. How does friendship with the world make one an adulterer?

12. Why would friendship with the world make one at enmity with God?

13. What does God yearn jealously over?

✦ 14. Considering the language of adultery and jealousy in these verses, what do you think God wants from us? See also these Old Testament references: Jeremiah 3:6-10 and Exodus 34:12-16.

✦ 15. What does this have to do with one's prayer life—asking and receiving?

♥ 16. How would you rate your wholehearted devotion to God, and conversely your friendship with the world?

♥ 17. What in this world tempts you to befriend it?

♥ 18. How can you increase your devotion to God and decrease your friendship with the world?

Read James 4:1-12.

James 4:6-10

◉ 1. Yesterday we examined our hearts and saw our friendship with the world is enmity with God. What hope does James give us at the beginning of verse 6?

✦ 2. What does it mean for God to give more grace?

◉ 3. How does God treat the proud, and how does he treat the humble? (James is quoting Proverbs 3:34.)

✦ 4. Using the chart below, list the commands in verses 7-10 and the results of obeying these commands.

Commands	Results of obedience

✦ 5. How do we resist the devil and draw near to God? Read Ephesians 6:10-18a.

✦ 6. Why do you think James tells his readers to be wretched, to mourn, to weep, and to turn their laughter to mourning and joy to gloom? What are they to be sad about?

✦ 7. What does this sadness have to do with humility? See also Matthew 5:3-5.

✦ 8. What does it mean to be exalted by God?

♥ 9. What are some ways you can humble yourself before the Lord?

♥ 10. What do you need to do to obey these commands in your life?

Day 4

Read James 4:1-12.

James 4:11-12

👁 1. What command does James give in verse 11?

👁 2. Why should one not speak evil against or judge a brother?

✦ 3. What law is James referring to? See also James 2:8-12.

👁 4. What are you if you judge the law?

👁 5. How many lawgivers and judges are there?

👁 6. Who is the lawgiver and judge?

✦ 7. In whose place are you putting yourself if you judge or speak evil against a brother?

✦ 8. Explain how a person speaking evil of a brother is usurping the place of God.

♥ 9. Examine your heart. Do you have a tendency to judge or speak evil of your sisters or brothers in Christ? In what ways do you struggle with this?

♥ 10. Read and pray through Ephesians 4:29-32.

Read James 4:1-12.

✦ 1. After reviewing the passage you studied this week, describe the problems James is addressing in the churches to whom he is writing.

✦ 2. How would you sum up in your own words the solutions James gives?

♥ 3. Think through any difficult situations you have faced in relationships with your brothers and sisters in Christ. How do James' solutions apply to help these situations?

♥ 4. If you are tempted to quarrel or fight in the future, how will you handle it?

Notes

Pray this week that you would trust the Lord with regard to your time and money.

Read James 4:13-16.

👁 1. Whom is James addressing in verse 13?

👁 2. What do they not know?

👁 3. How does James describe their lives?

👁 4. What ought they to say?

✛ 5. Who determines where we live and what we will do? See Acts 17:24-27 and Job 14:5. See also Proverbs 16:33, 1 Samuel 2:6-8, Ephesians 1:11, and Romans 8:28.

✛ 6. Sum up in your own words what James is teaching in verses 13-15.

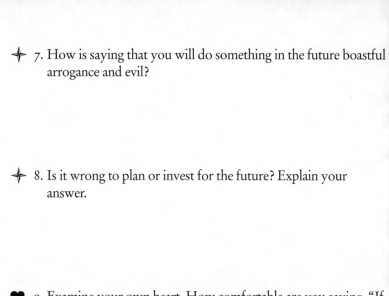

7. How is saying that you will do something in the future boastful arrogance and evil?

8. Is it wrong to plan or invest for the future? Explain your answer.

9. Examine your own heart. How comfortable are you saying, "If the Lord wills," when you make plans for the future?

10. Can you think of any verses that are comforting to you when your future is uncertain?

11. Pray for the Lord to write those verses on your heart and make you steadfast when you face uncertainty.

Read James 4:13-17.

✦ 1. Rewrite verse 17 in your own words.

✦ 2. Look at your summary of verses 13-15 from yesterday. How can our plans for tomorrow cause us to fail to do the right thing today?

♥ 3. Can you think of a specific time in your life when this has happened? Explain.

✦ 4. How does leaving the future in God's hands help us live rightly today?

♥ 5. In what area of your life are you struggling to make the most of your time and to leave the future to God? Consider areas like singleness, marriage, children, money, or health.

Day 3

Read James 5:1-6.

👁 1. Who is James addressing in this passage?

✦ 2. Do you think these rich people are believers or unbelievers? Why?

👁 3. What does James tell these rich people to do?

👁 4. Why should they weep and howl?

✦ 5. What is James saying about riches in verses 2-3?

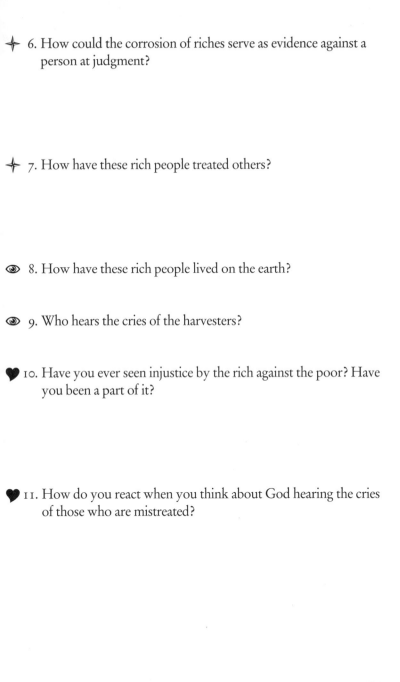

✦ 6. How could the corrosion of riches serve as evidence against a person at judgment?

✦ 7. How have these rich people treated others?

👁 8. How have these rich people lived on the earth?

👁 9. Who hears the cries of the harvesters?

❤ 10. Have you ever seen injustice by the rich against the poor? Have you been a part of it?

❤ 11. How do you react when you think about God hearing the cries of those who are mistreated?

♥ 12. Pray for more just treatment of the underprivileged. Also pray that Christian employers would be exemplary in their treatment of employees.

Day 4

Read James 5:1-6 and Matthew 6:19-21.

👁 1. What does Jesus command in Matthew 6:19?

👁 2. What happens to earthly treasure?

👁 3. What kind of treasure does Jesus tell us to store up?

✦ 4. According to the following verses, what is heavenly treasure?

    ✦ a) Isaiah 33:5-6

    ✦ b) Psalm 4:6-8

✦ c) Psalm 84:10-12

✦ 5. How does one store up treasure in heaven? Read 1 Timothy 6:17-19. See also 1 Corinthians 3:5-15.

👁 6. What doesn't happen to treasure in heaven?

👁 7. How are treasure and the heart connected?

✦ 8. What does it mean that where your treasure is, there your heart is also?

✦ 9. How does this passage in Matthew relate to our passage in James?

♥ 10. What do these passages say to you about your material possessions?

♥ 11. How are you storing up treasure in heaven?

Day 5

Read James 4:13-5:6.

✦ 1. Summarize the point of verses 4:13-17.

✦ 2. Summarize the point of verses 5:1-6.

✦ 3. How are these passages related to one another?

4. Spend some time thinking about how you use your time and money. How can you use these things to advance God's kingdom and store up treasure in heaven?

Pray this week for the Lord to increase your patience and steadfast faith in him.

Read James 5:7-12.

James 5:7-8

👁 1. To whom is James writing these verses?

👁 2. What does he tell them to do?

👁 3. What example does he use of patience?

✦ 4. In what way must a farmer be patient?

✦ 5. James repeats the admonition, "Be patient." What are these brothers to be patient about? (Consider the "therefore" in verse 7. What is the "therefore" there for?)

✦ 6. James says, "Establish your hearts." (The NIV translates it, "Stand firm.") What does this mean, and what does it have to do with patience?

✦ 7. What would patience look like for these beleaguered Christians?

◉ 8. What are these brothers to remain steadfast for (or when are they to remain steadfast until)?

✦ 9. What can these persecuted and mistreated Christians look forward to at the coming of the Lord?

♥ 10. What do you do when you are mistreated? In what worldly ways are you tempted to handle it: fight back, avoid the person, store it up and become bitter, gossip, take revenge in subtle ways?

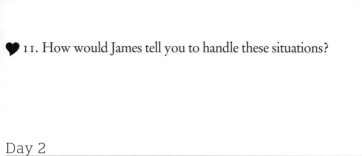 11. How would James tell you to handle these situations?

Day 2

Read James 5:7-12.

James 5:9

1. What command does James give in verse 9?

2. Who is doing the grumbling, and who is being grumbling against?

3. What ultimately is the consequence of grumbling against one another?

4. Who is standing at the door?

5. Why does it matter that the judge is standing at the door?

✦ 6. What does grumbling against one another have to do with the previous verses on patience and establishing one's heart?

✦ 7. Based on your answer to question 6 and your reading of James 3:5-12, why is grumbling against one another worthy of judgment?

♥ 8. In what situations do you tend to grumble? Do you take offense easily? Do you want things done your way in the church? Do you become easily frustrated with your weaker sister?

♥ 9. What can you do to fight against grumbling? How can you exercise more patience with your brothers and sisters in Christ?

Day 3

Read James 5:7-12.

James 5:10-11

1. Whom does James cite as an example of suffering and patience in verse 10?

2. Read Hebrews 11:32-38. How are these people an example for James' readers?

3. Can you think of a particular prophet or several prophets who were exemplary at suffering with patience?

4. Read Hebrews 11:13-16. What were the saints of old looking forward to that caused them to live by faith, even in the midst of great suffering?

5. What does James say of those who remain steadfast?

6. What does it mean to be blessed, and why do James and his readers consider those who remain steadfast blessed?

👁 7. Whom does James use as an example in verse 11?

✦ 8. How is Job an example of steadfastness? (Read Job 1:20-22, 2:9-10, 16:19, and 19:23-27.)

✦ 9. What is the purpose of the Lord in the suffering of James' readers (and, by extension, our suffering)? Remember James 1.

✦ 10. How does this purpose show that the Lord is compassionate and merciful?

♥ 11. Job was brought closer to God through his suffering and serves as an heroic example of trusting God in trials. Have you experienced trials that brought you closer to God as you trusted him through them? Explain.

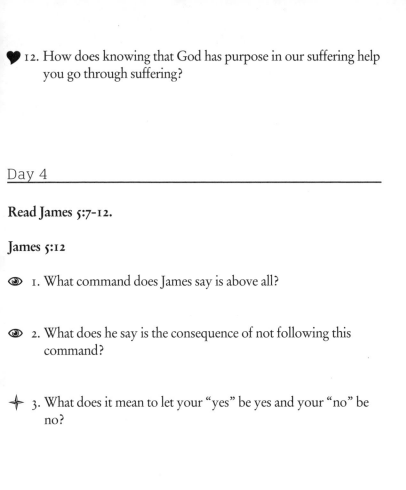

12. How does knowing that God has purpose in our suffering help you go through suffering?

Day 4

Read James 5:7-12.

James 5:12

1. What command does James say is above all?

2. What does he say is the consequence of not following this command?

3. What does it mean to let your "yes" be yes and your "no" be no?

4. Read Matthew 5:33-37. Sum up why Jesus prohibits taking oaths.

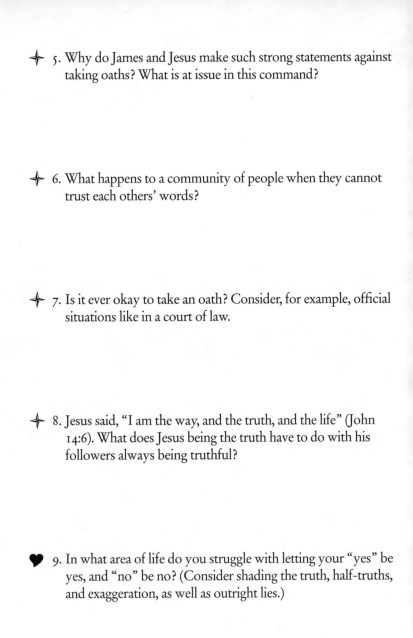

5. Why do James and Jesus make such strong statements against taking oaths? What is at issue in this command?

6. What happens to a community of people when they cannot trust each others' words?

7. Is it ever okay to take an oath? Consider, for example, official situations like in a court of law.

8. Jesus said, "I am the way, and the truth, and the life" (John 14:6). What does Jesus being the truth have to do with his followers always being truthful?

9. In what area of life do you struggle with letting your "yes" be yes, and "no" be no? (Consider shading the truth, half-truths, and exaggeration, as well as outright lies.)

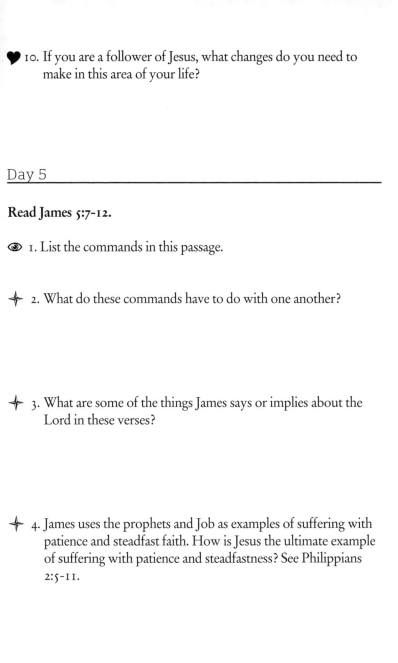

10. If you are a follower of Jesus, what changes do you need to make in this area of your life?

Day 5

Read James 5:7-12.

1. List the commands in this passage.

2. What do these commands have to do with one another?

3. What are some of the things James says or implies about the Lord in these verses?

4. James uses the prophets and Job as examples of suffering with patience and steadfast faith. How is Jesus the ultimate example of suffering with patience and steadfastness? See Philippians 2:5-11.

✦ 5. How are the commands you listed above a fitting response to what Jesus has done?

♥ 6. As you consider Jesus, who in compassion and mercy gave his life to create a people for himself and who is coming again to judge the world, what is your response?

Begin your study each day praying for the Lord to make you into a righteous woman of prayer.

Read James 5:13-20.

James 5:13-14

👁 1. James asks and responds to three questions in this passage. Fill in the following chart:

	Question	Response
👁 a.		
👁 b.		
👁 c.		

✦ 2. What do the responses to these questions have in common?

✦ 3. What do you think the suffering person should pray for? Are there any verses you have studied previously in James that help you answer this question?

♥ 4. How do you handle suffering in your life?

♥ 5. What do you pray for when you are going through suffering?

♥ 6. What about when you are cheerful? Do you sing praise? Explain your answer.

♥ 7. If you are a follower of Jesus, pray for yourself and your sisters in Christ to be women who ask God for wisdom and steadfastness when going through times of suffering and who sing praise during times of cheerfulness.

Read James 5:13-20.

James 5:14-15

◉ 1. What does James tell one who is sick to do?

◉ 2. What are the elders to do?

✦ 3. What is an elder of the church? See Titus 1:5-9.

✦ 4. Why do you think the elders were to anoint the sick person with oil in addition to praying? See Mark 6:13 and Luke 10:34.

Note: There are basically two views about the purpose of the oil. One is that it is medicinal. In the time of Jesus, oil was used by doctors and others for its healing properties. We see this use in the story of the Good Samaritan (Luke 10:34). The other view is that the oil represents the power of the Holy Spirit to heal the sick. Many commentators take a middle ground, noting that the oil may have had a practical use but may also have been symbolic of the Holy Spirit. One thing we know for sure, God is the author of healing whether it is by medicine or by miracle.

👁 5. In whose name do the elders pray and anoint with oil?

✦ 6. What does this suggest or reinforce about who is doing the healing?

✦ 7. Whose prayer of faith saves the sick person, and what does this suggest about whether healing is tied to the amount of faith of the sick person?

👁 8. What three things does James say will happen as a result of the prayer of faith?

✦ 9. Do you think these three things are focused on physical healing, or do they suggest something else also? Explain your answer.

❤ 10. What does James' emphasis here on prayer, salvation, and forgiveness suggest about what we should be focused on during times of illness?

♥ 11. What does this emphasis suggest about how the church should be focused in the life of someone with an illness?

Day 3

Read James 5:13-20.

James 5:15b-16a

👁 1. In verse 15 James seems to move from sickness to sinfulness. What does James say will be the benefits for the sick person if the elders pray?

✦ 2. Why do you think sickness and sin seem to be connected here?

✦ 3. How do sickness and sin relate to one another? Read John 5:14 and John 9:3.

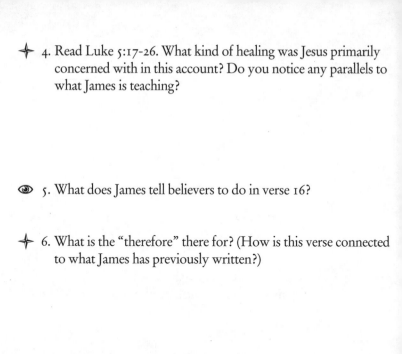

4. Read Luke 5:17-26. What kind of healing was Jesus primarily concerned with in this account? Do you notice any parallels to what James is teaching?

5. What does James tell believers to do in verse 16?

6. What is the "therefore" there for? (How is this verse connected to what James has previously written?)

7. What is the result of confessing sins to one another and praying for one another?

8. What kind of healing do you think James is writing about in verse 16?

9. Why should we in the church confess our sins to one another? Why not just keep them private? Why not just confess them to God?

♥ 10. Why should we in the church care about one another's sin enough to pray for each other?

♥ 11. Do you have sisters in Christ you can confess your sins to, who will pray for you and keep you accountable? If not, why not? If so, how can you better use your sisters as a gift from God to help you fight sin?

Day 4

Read James 5:13-20.

James 5:16b-18

👁 1. What does James write about the prayer of a righteous person?

👁 2. Whom does James use as an example of a righteous person praying?

✦ 3. Summarize what James says about Elijah.

✦ 4. Read 1 Kings 17-18. What do you notice about Elijah's responses to God in these chapters?

✦ 5. What makes Elijah a righteous man?

✦ 6. James writes, "Elijah was a man with a nature like ours." Why do you think James includes that comment about Elijah?

✦ 7. After reading about the example of Elijah, how would you describe a righteous person?

♥ 8. How can you apply Elijah's example to your life?

♥ 9. Are your prayers being used by God in the lives of others? Who are you regularly praying for in the church?

Day 5

Read carefully through all of James.

✢ 1. Jot down the major themes of the letter.

✢ 2. The style of the conclusion of James' letter is different from other New Testament letters. There is no benediction or blessing, and there are no final greetings. Summarize James' closing two verses.

✢ 3. What does it mean for someone to wander from the truth? (Remember the context of James.)

✦ 4. How does one bring back a sinner from his wandering?

✦ 5. Explain how this saves a sinner's soul and covers sins.

✦ 6. This act of bringing a sinner back requires judging that person's actions as sinful and confronting that person with the sin, but James in 4:11-12 writes against judging and speaking against a brother. How should we reconcile these two statements?

✦ 7. Looking back at the major themes of the letter of James you noted above, how are verses 19 and 20 a fitting end to the letter?

♥ 8. Examine your life. Are you involved enough in the lives of others in the church to see their sin? Are you in close enough relationship with others to have earned their trust so that you can speak to them about sin in their lives?

♥ 9. What about sin in your life? Are you known well enough by others in the church for them to see your sin? Are you humble enough to examine yourself if a sister in Christ does confront your sin?

♥ 10. Paul Tripp has said, "Your walk with God is a community project." In fact, he writes in his book, *How People Change*, "The ultimate goal of God's grace is an active, healthy, unified body of believers, a full-fledged family freed from sin and its slavery." (Timothy S. Lane and Paul David Tripp, *How People Change* [Greensboro, NC: New Growth Press, 2006], p 75) We've seen this goal of God expressed in very practical ways throughout this study of James as he addresses how we in the church should treat one another. As we end the study, what action do you need to take to increase your commitment to meaningful relationships in the body of Christ that help you to grow?

Lord God Almighty,
I ask not to be enrolled amongst the earthly great and rich,
    but to be numbered with the spiritually blessed.
Make it my present, supreme, persevering concern
    to obtain those blessings which are
        spiritual in their nature,
        eternal in their continuance,
        satisfying in their possession.
Preserve me from a false estimate of the whole
    or a part of my character;
May I pay my regard to
    my principles as well as my conduct,
    my motives as well as my actions.
Help me
    never to mistake the excitement of my passions
        for the renewing of the Holy Spirit,
    never to judge my religion by occasional impressions and impulses,
        but by my constant and prevailing disposition.
May my heart be right with thee,
    and my life as becometh the gospel.
May I maintain a supreme regard to another and better world,
    and feel and confess myself a stranger and a pilgrim here.
Afford me all the direction, defence, support,
    and consolation my journey hence requires,
    and grant me a mind stayed upon thee.
Give me large abundance of the supply of the Spirit of Jesus,
    that I may be prepared for every duty,
    love thee in all my mercies.
    submit to thee in every trial,
    trust thee when walking in darkness,
    have peace in thee amidst life's changes.
Lord, I believe, help thou my unbelief
    and uncertainties.

—"True Religion," *The Valley of Vision* (Carlisle, PA: Banner of Truth, 2002) p 118

Also from Cruciform Press

Some of our most relevant books are featured on the following pages. But make sure you also see these other outstanding titles:

Friends and Lovers: Cultivating Companionship & Intimacy in Marriage, by Joel R. Beeke

Grieving, Hope, and Solace: When a Loved One Dies in Christ, by Albert N. Martin

Broken Vows: Divorce and the Goodness of God, by John Greco

Servanthood as Worship: The Privelige of Life in the Local Church, by Nate Palmer

Cruciform: Living the Cross-Shaped Life, by Jimmy Davis

Innocent Blood: Challenging the Powers of Death with the Gospel of Life, by John Ensor

Reclaiming Adoption: Missional Living Through the Rediscovery of Abba Father, by Dan Cruver, John Piper, Scotty Smith, Richard D. Phillips, Jason Kovacs

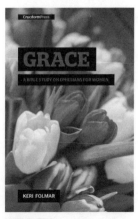

GRACE: A Bible Study
on Ephesians for Women

bit.ly/GraceStudy

JOY! – A Bible Study on
Philippians for Women

bit.ly/JoyStudy

Inductive Bible studies for women by Keri Folmar
endorsed by...

Kathleen Nielson is author of the *Living Word Bible Studies;* Director of Women's Initiatives, The Gospel Coalition; and wife of Niel, who served as President of Covenant College from 2002 to 2012.

Diane Schreiner is the mother of four grown children and has led women's Bible studies for more than 20 years. She is the wife of Tom Schreiner, an author and pastor who serves at Southern Baptist Theological Seminary as Professor of New Testament Interpretation, Professor of Biblical Theology, and Associate Dean of the School of Theology.

Connie Dever is author of *The Praise Factory* children's ministry curriculum and wife of Pastor Mark Dever, President of 9 Marks Ministries

Kristie Anyabwile, holds a history degree from NC State University, and is married to Thabiti, Assistant Pastor for Church Planting at Capitol Hill Baptist Church in Washington DC, and a Council Member for The Gospel Coalition.

Gloria Furman is a pastor's wife in the Middle East and author of *Glimpses of Grace* and *Treasuring Christ When Your Hands Are Full.*

"It is hard to imagine a better inductive Bible study tool than this one."
– Diane Schreiner

Knowable Word

Helping Ordinary People Learn to Study the Bible

by Peter Krol
Foreword by Tedd Tripp

Observe...Interpret...Apply

Simple concepts at the heart of good Bible study. Learn the basics in a few minutes—gain skills for a lifetime. The spiritual payoff is huge.

Ready?

117 pages — Learn more at bit.ly/Knowable

"*Knowable Word* is valuable for those who have never done in-depth Bible study and a good review for those who have. I look forward to using this book to improve my own Bible study....a great service."
Jerry Bridges, author and speaker

"It is hard to over-estimate the value of this tidy volume. It is clear and uncomplicated. No one will be off-put by this book. It will engage the novice and the serious student of Scripture. It works as a solid read for individuals or as an exciting study for a small group."
Tedd Tripp, pastor and author (from the Foreword)

"At the heart of *Knowable Word* is a glorious and crucial conviction: that understanding the Bible is not the preserve of a few, but the privilege and joy of all God's people. Peter Krol's book demystifies the process of reading God's Word and in so doing enfranchises the people of God. I warmly encourage you to read it. Better still, read it with others and apply its method together."
Dr. Tim Chester, The Porterbrook Network

"Here is an excellent practical guide to interpreting the Bible. Krol has thought through, tested, and illustrated in a clear, accessible way basic steps in interpreting the Bible, and made everything available in a way that will encourage ordinary people to deepen their own study."
Vern Poythress, Westminster Theological Seminary

"Knowable Word does a tremendous service. It gives us tools to dig into the Bible that go far beyond the most common light and superficial methods. This book is biblically rooted, theologically rich, time-tested, and extremely applicable. Read and use it in your own study, and give it to others in your life and ministry. Enjoy the feast!"
L Stephen Lutz, pastor, author of College Ministry in a Post-Christian Culture

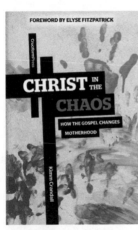

FOREWORD BY ELYSE FITZPATRICK

CHRIST IN THE CHAOS

HOW THE GOSPEL CHANGES MOTHERHOOD

Kimm Crandall

Christ in the Chaos
How the Gospel Changes Motherhood

by Kimm Crandall

FOREWORD BY ELYSE FITZPATRICK

MOMS:
- **Stop comparing yourself to others.**
- **Stop striving to meet false expectations.**
- **Stop thinking your performance dictates your worth.**
- **Instead, look to the gospel for rest, joy, sufficiency, identity, and motivation.**

Learn more at bit.ly/Christ-in

"Although Kimm Crandall's message would revive any soul longing for the breath of the gospel of grace, I am especially eager to recommend this book to that heart who strives to know God and to make him known to the little ones who call her 'Momma.' Kimm is a candid and gracious fellow sojourner, faithfully pointing to God's immeasurable steadfast love and grace in the midst of our mess."

Lauren Chandler, wife of Matt Chandler (pastor of The Village Church), mother of three, writer, singer, and speaker

"What an amazingly wild and wise, disruptive and delighting, freeing and focusing book. Kimm's book is for every parent willing to take the stewardship of children and the riches of the gospel seriously. This is one of the most helpful and encouraging books on parenting I've read in the past twenty years. Kimm writes as a multi-child mom and a grace-saturated woman who understands the exhausting demands of good parenting and the inexhaustible supply of God's grace. This will be a book you will want to give to parents, to-be parents, and grandparents."

Scotty Smith, author; Founding Pastor, Christ Community Church

"Kimm Crandall has discovered that chaos can be the perfect context in which to experience God's liberating grace. She is a wise, practical, gospel-drenched guide for anyone navigating through the wearisome terrain of parenting."

Tullian Tchividjian, author; Pastor, Coral Ridge Presbyterian Church

"Kimm gives us the truth of free grace that unshackles us from trying to be Mom of the Year, and shows us how the gospel changes motherhood from drudgery to joy. I pray each mom who finds this book becomes more aware of how Christ's love for her changes everything about her."

Jessica Thompson, coauthor of Give them Grace

The Organized Heart
A Woman's Guide to Conquering Chaos

by Staci Eastin

Disorganized?

You don't need more rules, the latest technique, or a new gadget.

This book will show you a different, better way. A way grounded in the grace of God.

Learn more at bit.ly/OHEART

"Staci Eastin packs a gracious punch, full of insights about our disorganized hearts and lives, immediately followed by the balm of gospel-shaped hopes. This book is ideal for accountability partners and small groups."

Carolyn McCulley, blogger, filmmaker, author of Radical Womahood and Did I Kiss Marriage Goodbye?

"Unless we understand the spiritual dimension of productivity, our techniques will ultimately backfire. Find that dimension here. Encouraging and uplifting rather than guilt-driven, this book can help women who want to be more organized but know that adding a new method is not enough."

Matt Perman, former Director of Strategy at Desiring God, blogger, author of the forthcoming, What's Best Next: How the Gospel Transforms the Way You Get Things Done

"Organizing a home can be an insurmountable challenge for a woman. The Organized Heart makes a unique connection between idols of the heart and the ability to run a well-managed home. This is not a how-to. Eastin looks at sin as the root problem of disorganization. She offers a fresh new approach and one I recommend, especially to those of us who have tried all the other self-help models and failed."

Aileen Challies, Mom of three; wife of blogger, author, and pastor Tim Challies

FROM READER REVIEWS:

"Undoubtedly the first and most important book any Christian woman who wants to start living a disciplined and organized life should read." **BeckyPliego.com**

"This is a powerful book that is far from the ordinary 'how to' organizing fare." **Melissa Nixon Jackson**

"This is a book that I can't recommend highly enough." **Samantha Muthia, DomesticKingdom.com**

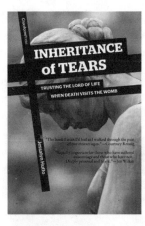

Inheritance of Tears
Trusting the Lord of Life When Death
Visits the Womb

by Jessalyn Hutto

**Miscarriage: Deeply traumatic, tragically
common...and so often misunderstood or
trivialized.**

**The gospel can make all the difference to
suffering mothers.**

Learn more at bit.ly/OFTEARS

"We wish there had been good Christian books on miscarriage available when we
faced that terrible trial. This book is written out of deep suffering, but with an even
deeper sense of hope. This book can help you think and pray if you have faced
miscarriage, and it can help you understand how to minister to someone who has.
grieving women in your local church."
   Russel and Maria Moore, Russel Moore is President of the Ethics and Religious
   Liberty Commission of the Southern Baptist Convention

"This book is equally important for those who have suffered miscarriage and those
who have not. Rarely is the topic of miscarriage addressed with such candor and
depth. Deeply personal and brave.... May her words minister to many."
   Jen Wilkin, author, *Women of the Word* (Crossway)

"Comforting, biblical, helpful...a needed word for anyone who has experienced this
great loss. A great resource for the church."
   Trillia Newbell, author of *Fear and Faith* (2015) and *United* (2014)

"Many women grasp for hope in the overwhelming days of grief that follow miscarriage. I have twice been that woman, and Jessalyn Hutto has written the book I wish I'd
had as I walked through the pain. This book will be a healing balm to grieving women."
   Courtney Reissig, wife; mom; author, The Accidental Feminist

"Miscarriage? Don't talk about it. Sadly, this is the approach many churches take. As a
result, the woman in the pew suffers unbearable pain and grieves all alone. Change
must happen, and Inheritance of Tears is the place to start.."
   Matthew Barrett, Executive Editor, Credo Magazine

"She guides us theologically, so that we see God's wisdom, God's purpose, and God's
love in the midst of our suffering. I gladly recommend this work to others."
   Tom Schreiner, The Southern Baptist Theological Seminary

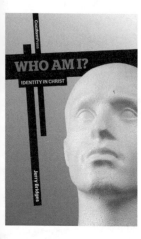

Who Am I?
Identity in Christ

by Jerry Bridges

Jerry Bridges unpacks Scripture to give the Christian eight clear, simple, interlocking answers to one of the most essential questions of life.

Also available as an audiobook read by Alistair Begg

Learn more at bit.ly/WHOAMI

"Jerry Bridges' gift for simple but deep spiritual communication is fully displayed in this warm-hearted, biblical spelling out of the Christian's true identity in Christ."

> **J.I. Packer, *Theological Editor*, ESV Study Bible; *author*, Knowing God, A Quest for Godliness, Concise Theology**

"I know of no one better prepared than Jerry Bridges to write *Who Am I?* He is a man who knows who he is in Christ and he helps us to see succinctly and clearly who we are to be. Thank you for another gift to the Church of your wisdom and insight in this book."

> **R.C. Sproul, *founder, chairman, president, Ligonier Ministries; executive editor,* Tabletalk *magazine; general editor,* The Reformation Study Bible**

"*Who Am I?* answers one of the most pressing questions of our time in clear gospel categories straight from the Bible. This little book is a great resource to ground new believers and remind all of us of what God has made us through faith in Jesus. Thank the Lord for Jerry Bridges, who continues to provide the warm, clear, and biblically balanced teaching that has made him so beloved to this generation of Christians."

> **Richard D. Phillips, *Senior Minister, Second Presbyterian Church, Greenville, SC***

TABLE OF CONTENTS

The Company We Keep
In Search of Biblical Friendship

by Jonathan Holmes
Foreword by Ed Welch

Biblical friendship is deep, honest, pure, tranparent, and liberating.

It is also attainable.

112 pages
Learn more at bit.ly/B-Friend

"Jonathan Holmes has the enviable ability to say a great deal in a few words. Here is a wonderful primer on the nature of biblical friendship—what it means and why it matters."
Alistair Begg, Truth for Life; Senior Pastor, Parkside Church,

"Jonathan has succeeded in giving us a picture of how normal, daily, biblical friendships can be used by God to mold us into the likeness of Christ. If you want a solid, fresh way of re-thinking all of your relationships, read this book."
Dr. Tim S. Lane, co-author, How People Change

"A robust and relevant GPS for intentional and vulnerable gospel-centered friendships...a great book not only for individuals, but also for small groups...a significant contribution to the Kingdom."
Robert W. Kellemen, Exec. Dir., Biblical Counseling Coalition

"Short. Thoughtful. Biblical. Practical. I'm planning to get my friends to read this book so we can transform our friendships."
Deepak Reju, Pastor of Biblical Counseling, Capitol Hill Baptist

"Practical guidance that is both biblical and inspiring. I'll be recommending this book to friends and counselees."
Winston T. Smith, faculty, Christian Counseling and Educational Foundation

"I talk with many Christians who have intensely practical questions about how to make and maintain friendships with their fellow believers. Jonathan Holmes' book is filled with answers that are equally down-to-earth, nitty-gritty, and specific. This is a book that isn't just a roadmap for cultivating Christian friendship. It's also a tour guide, taking us where we need to go with warmth and wisdom."
Wesley Hill, assistant professor of biblical studies, Trinity School for Ministry, Ambridge, Pennsylvania and author of Washed and Waiting